HEARING 101

Encountering God Series
Book 2

HEARING 101

FAITH D. BLATCHFORD

Cover Design © Brad Webster
Interior © Lorraine Box

ISBN # 978-0-9896477-0-0

Published by AGE TO COME
www.faithblatchford.com

Printed in the United States of America

FOREWORD

Every believer holds possession of the precious voice of Jesus. He speaks unceasing Truth forever. For our part, we follow His lead, but this begins with an attuned ear. If you are not hearing His voice, this book is for you.

Jesus did not tolerate deafness, especially the spiritual kind. Spiritual deafness is a modern Christian malady that is correctable and unnecessary. We can — in fact must — live with an ongoing dialogue between ourselves and our Maker. To do otherwise leaves a life hollow. Such is the inheritance for the enemies of heaven and not the Children of God.

This small book is written in such honesty, the reader finds him or her self immersed in the practicum of truth. Faith Blatchford shares her wisdom in short easily read chapters. Her writing style is authentic, her goal clear, and understandable. Like most great writers, she has simplified a mystery and made it easy for the reader to activate. But most important, Faith has written a book that you can immediately put to work with hearing God's voice.

I count it an honor to name Faith Blatchford as a friend. Her gentle poise and sound wisdom is shared through the lines in this book. As an author and teacher, I find Faith Blatchford to demonstrate power wrapped in a disarming cover — but don't be deceived. Faith Blatchford drives to the very heart of the Father. Her approach is direct, her language fresh, her message profound. In short, this book breathes life into the faith-seed residing inside you. Water that seed with *Hearing 101* and grow strong under the tutelage of His voice!

Stephen K. De Silva, CPA

Bethel Church, Redding, California, CFO
Author of *Money and the Prosperous Soul,*
Tipping the Scales of Favor and Blessing

DEDICATION

L earning to hear God has been a life-long journey. I am thankful for fellow travellers along the way who have demonstrated a life of conversation with God and provided practical tools for building the same kind of relationship in my own life. This book is dedicated to several people in particular, whose influence enabled me to start a life-changing daily dialogue with my Father.

The Sozo tools developed for the Bethel Sozo ministry, by Dawna DeSilva and Teresa Liebscher, helped me discover and remove some of the blocks in my life which kept me from hearing God. Most of the wax in my ears was an accumulation of lies either about God or about myself. Once the lies were uncovered and replaced by the Truth, my hearing improved.

The tone of God's voice changed dramatically through revelation about Bill Johnson's statement, "Jesus is perfect theology." I no longer heard the voice of an angry, punishing God, but rather the heart of a loving Father who allowed His Son to be punished instead of me.

Kris Vallotton and Doug Addison taught me the importance of risk and practice as integral parts of increasing my confidence in hearing. Their teaching brought hearing God out of the mystical realm into the everyday world in which I live.

Many thanks to these friends who have enriched my relationship with my Father and enabled me to help others improve the quality of their communication with Him as well.

CONTENTS

PREFACE

When I was 10, I had a close friend who lived next door. We spent every waking moment together. One day we discovered a perfect place to build a fort. Everything about it was top secret. Only our closest friends were trusted with the location and password. Even at that age, we knew friendship had privileges. Knowledge of the secrets was a result of the relationship.

When I became a believer at 15, I was thrilled Jesus would include me in His circle of friends. Jesus calls His disciples friends, not servants. Friends are privy to intimate information. Servants receive nothing but specific details to do their job. The possibility of being God's friend intrigued me. I realized all my friends talked to me. It made sense if God was my friend, He would talk to me too.

God spoke to me before I committed my life to Christ. One night I sensed His presence as I lay on a boat deck looking at the sky shining with billions of stars. I was trying to sort out whether I believed there was a God. Through the dramatic display in the sky that night He convinced me He existed.

Another night I was sick and alone in a tiny bedroom of a cabin situated on the side of a mountain in the French Alps. I spoke very little French and the owners of the house even less English. The rest of the group with whom I was travelling was on a camping trip with our French teacher. As I lay crying, wishing I hadn't begged my parents to let me come on the trip, I heard singing through the open window. Although I couldn't understand the words, the rich tones of the harmonies comforted me. Later I learned a group of Catholic priests were staying at a campsite up the mountain. God used their singing to speak peace to me.*

God is always speaking. He has a myriad of ways to do so. Sadly, not everyone experiences communication with God as His friend. Often people tell me they are able to hear God for others but can't hear Him speak to them personally. Others simply can't hear God at all. Both groups feel discouragement and condemnation. If you are in either group, this book is for you. I believe by the end of it you will hear God whispering secrets in your ear!

* First appeared in *Voices of Revival*

HEARING...

a matter of life and death

Hearing is not optional. God commands it. The reason He does, is for our good, not His. He patiently works with us to develop good listening skills. Sometimes hearing lessons come at inconvenient times.

One evening I was exhausted and ready to go to sleep on the couch in the living room at my mother's house. She had fallen and bruised her ribs. I was spending the night in case she needed help. The couch was uncomfortable, but the atmosphere in the room was restful as I looked out on the dimly lit garden through the floor-to-ceiling glass windows.

My thoughts were interrupted by the still small

voice inside saying, "Go get your purse and shoes. Put them under the couch." My first response was to push the "ignore" button. The Holy Spirit doesn't recognize "ignore." Once again I heard, "Go get your purse and shoes." After the third time, begrudgingly, I walked to the back of the house where I had left my belongings. As I placed the purse and shoes under the couch, I wanted to say, "There. Are you satisfied?" but decided not to.

Without any further delay, I fell asleep to the sound of Mother's intermittent snoring from her bedroom down the hall. My sleep was rudely interrupted by the terrifying sound of vibrating windows being violently shaken. Although still groggy, I knew instantly the swinging chandelier and rolling movement in the dark room were not remnants of a dream. This was a southern California earthquake.

The next day the event was officially named the *Northridge Earthquake.* If you live in California, you become accustomed to periodic temblors. This one was above normal. It was a 6.7 magnitude quake which injured 9000 people, caused $40 billion in damage, and produced the strongest ground motion ever recorded in a U.S. city. My mother lived 50 miles from the epicenter of the quake. It was a frightening experience, even though nothing was damaged in the house. The pictures of the destruction, as well as reports from friends, were unsettling.

For the next several days the house swayed and the windows shook with wave after wave of aftershocks. My anxiety increased with each one. It was difficult to sleep at night. No one could predict if the 6.7 quake was a precursor of the "big one." Then I heard the still small voice again. "I warned you and I will always warn you ahead of time."

For the first time since the first shaking, I remembered being nudged to get my purse and shoes. The dots connected. As a school administrator in southern California, I had been required to attend earthquake preparation training. One recommendation was to keep your purse and shoes under your bed at night in case a rapid evacuation of the house was needed. Having those two items nearby and protected from broken glass caused by the quake could be a lifesaver.

The most terrifying aspect of an earthquake is its suddenness. No one has invented an early warning system. There are high-tech systems to alert coastal areas about approaching hurricanes, but nothing similar for the unexpected shift of the plates under the earth's surface. The Northridge quake taught me an important lesson. The Holy Spirit can warn me of events before they happen. If I not only listen but obey His instructions, it could save my life. If I had been near the epicenter of the Northridge quake, it would have been vitally important to have my shoes and bag under the couch.

The hearing lessons continued and with each one, the stakes were higher. Several years later I moved from California to a barrier island 17 miles long and four miles wide on the Atlantic Ocean in south Georgia. Instead of earthquakes, this area is known for hurricanes. The hurricane season starts June first and continues until November thirtieth. I thought it would be much more relaxing living in Georgia than southern California because hurricanes never take you by surprise. However, instead of a jolt of fear, I experienced days and days of increasing anxiety as I watched the Weather Channel's "cone of uncertainty" heading towards the island.

Floyd, a Category Four hurricane, measured over 500 miles in diameter. The storm surge was predicted to be 20 feet high. That much water would have completely submerged the island. Our city appeared to be the bull's-eye for the storm. We were ordered to leave the island. The approaching hurricane caused the largest peacetime evacuation in the history of the United States. My friends helped me pack pictures, documents, sentimental objects as well as oxygen tanks for my elderly mother, the recliner in which she slept, and suitcases of clothes for what might be an extended stay at a hotel. Before screwing on the last storm shutter, we stood in my bedroom to pray. I was not feeling great faith. My heart was pounding and my mind racing with catastrophic scenarios even as I mouthed words asking for protection.

In the midst of my panic, I had a vision of the beach and Atlantic Ocean less than a mile from the house. The scene was dark. Huge, menacing waves and white caps crashed on the beach. Standing on the crest of a wave with His back to the shore was Jesus. His hand was raised as if giving a hand signal to the wind to stop. Even though I was trembling with fear at the thought of the approaching storm, I knew it was not going to affect the island. Jesus had told it to "Be Still."

We got in the car and drove inland along with thousands of others. A normal three and one-quarter hours drive took over six hours because of the evacuation. The next day I called my neighbor.

He had decided he would not leave, but rather "go down with the island." The phone call went through as if there had been no storm. That was my first clue that Jesus standing on the water offshore had averted the disaster. My neighbor told me there was no damage and it was safe to come home.

Not too long after Floyd's visit, another storm began to move across the Atlantic from the coast of Africa. As I watched the weather report, I identified again with the story of the disciples on a boat in the middle of a raging storm. Now it was time for me to do more than read about Jesus speaking to the storm. I was required to do what I had read and had seen. My first attempt to speak to a storm was hesitant as I stood on the end of the dock facing the pounding Atlantic surf. As I spoke peace to the approaching storm, I heard Father God say, "It's not going to damage the island." It didn't.

Hurricanes are given names starting with the first letter of the alphabet. One season there were so many named storms, every letter of the alphabet was used. Midway through the summer I had planned a trip to visit friends who lived three and one-quarter hours due west from me. Another named hurricane had our island in it's crosshairs. I had gone to the beach and spoken peace to the storm. Once again I heard God's voice saying, "It's not going to damage the island."

The night before my trip, the weather station showed the storm still headed toward the island. I decided to pack the car that night. Stacked in one corner of my room were boxes full of important documents, pictures, and valuables. Standard procedure in hurricane country is to have those irreplaceable items packed in case it becomes necessary to evacuate. There was room in the trunk of my station wagon, so I decided to take them with me.

As I put the first box in the car I heard Father God ask, "What are you doing?" When He asks a question like that, He is not doing it to get information. He already knows everything. I said, "I am putting this box in the car in case the hurricane comes while I am gone." He responded, "Didn't you just speak peace to the storm?" I answered affirmatively. He asked me if I had heard His response to my declaration to the storm. Once again my answer was "yes." I knew I was at a crossroads.

He made the choice even more clear. He said, "If you take the boxes, you will lose everything. If you leave them, you will keep everything." This was not a life-or-death situation, but definitely more serious than the shoes under the couch. I thought for a few minutes, replaying the various conversations with God. The voice I had heard speaking to me was His. I took the box from the car and placed it back with the others in the corner of the room. All the hearing lessons of previous years had prepared me for that decision. The hurricane never touched the island.

As my ear training continued, I was inspired by three men in the Old Testament. They stand out because of their capacity to hear God speak to them under the pressure of life-and-death situations. Their hearing saved not only their own lives but the lives of family, friends, and even nations.

Noah was an ordinary married man, with children, who had a relationship with God. One day he heard God tell him to build a boat. Noah was not a boat builder by trade. He may never have even seen a boat. If he had, it is unlikely it was the size of the one he was commissioned to construct. God gave him the details he needed to build a 500-foot ship. The instructions included a list of the cargo he was to collect and carry. He was told the boat would keep him and his family safe from drowning in the impending flood. Once the ark was completed, God announced the rain would start in seven days. It did.

The building project took approximately 100 years. Noah was the only one who had heard the warning about the flood. His faith that he had heard God's voice was strong enough to convince his family to stay committed to the task. Their belief the flood was coming kept them sawing, hammering, and painting year after year in spite of ridicule that must have been hurled at them.

In addition to neighborhood scoffers, I am sure at times Noah had to deal with his children's lagging enthusiasm as well as his wife's exasperation with the endless amount of sawdust blowing into their tent. Noah's confidence in his communication with God was strong enough to withstand any opposition. He knew the voice. His obedience to the words he heard saved him and his family from death by drowning.

Daniel is another Bible hero who survived certain death because he heard the voice of God. He was faced with a life-threatening challenge while living in Babylon during the reign of King Nebuchadnezzar. The king needed someone to interpret a dream for him. Unfortunately for the magicians, the king had forgotten it. None of the wise men in Babylon were able to tell the king his dream. His fury at their ineffectiveness resulted in a decree to kill them all.

Before the order was carried out, Daniel told the king he would give him the dream and the interpretation. The king was willing to grant Daniel additional time. Daniel and his three friends used the time to pray, trusting God would reveal the secret and save their lives. God gave Daniel revelation in a dream which he shared with the king. His ability to hear God through a night vision saved his life. In addition, he and his friends were promoted to positions of authority in the governing of Babylon.

Although the stakes were high for Noah and Daniel to hear God, the pressure was even greater on Joseph. None of the magicians in Egypt could interpret the Pharaoh's dream. Joseph's only hope of being released from the dungeon was his ability to explain the meaning of the dream. Joseph's future, as well as that of the entire nation of Egypt, rested on his capacity to hear God. He was given the correct interpretation of the Pharaoh's dream. The relationship he enjoyed with God enabled him to administrate a 14-year economic plan that brought prosperity to Egypt. The wisdom he received saved his family from starvation, as well as the people of

Egypt and neighboring nations.

These three men had years of training. They learned to hear God in the little things. Their friendship with God was the bridge over which the information traveled. When their lives were on the line, they had confidence in their ability to recognize the sound of their Friend's voice. We may not need to hear God in order to save a nation, but we may need to hear Him to save ourselves or our family in a crisis.

DOES GOD
REALLY WANT
TO TALK TO ME?

The Bible is the written record of God's words to man. It contains 773,692 words. John wrote in his Gospel (John 21:25) the world wasn't large enough to contain a written record of all the *miracles* done by Jesus. I don't believe the universe has sufficient space to house the books required to record all of God's *words* from creation to the present. Hebrews 1:1 gives perspective on the length and breadth of God's communication with us.

Hebrews 1:1-2

God, who at various times and in various ways

25

spoke in time past unto the fathers by the prophets, has in these last days spoken to us by [His] son.

If it were possible to gather all the words spoken by men and women from the beginning of creation, it is probable God's word count would surpass man's.

Genesis 1:3 records the fact that the first words ever spoken in creation were by God. It isn't so much what He said that is important, but the fact that the start of all life began with God speaking. He could have blown, whistled, clapped, danced, pointed, or roared. He's God and as God He does whatever He wants. In this case He wanted to speak.

From the moment He started speaking, He has not stopped. John 1:1 says, "In the beginning was the Word and the Word was with God and the Word was God." It is difficult for God *not* to speak because Word is the essence of who He is.

God initiated the conversation with man. Once He had created Adam and Eve, He spoke to them. His desire was for two-way communication. His breath blowing into Adam's mouth provided the necessary air passing over the vocal cords for Adam to speak. God is the initiator of everything in our life. We cannot even communicate apart from Him.

Just because God proves He is a talker does not deal with my fear that He doesn't want to talk to me. It is easy to believe He wanted to talk to the Bible heroes as well as today's famous Christians. Because God created me and knows everything about me, He knew in advance I would have difficulty believing He would include me among His friends.

God implements the skills a successful lawyer would use to persuade a jury in a court of law. His goal is to prove His desire to speak to everyone, including me. The first evidence He uses in the case is the record of His speaking to things which didn't even exist. Paul records God's words to the nonexistent ones:

Romans 4:17

...God, who gives life to the dead and calls those things which do not exist as though they did.

If He spoke to nothing, it is probable He would speak to something. If I am a something, it would be safe to assume He would speak to me.

God continues to make His case. In the Old

Testament He spoke to people directly, either through angels or through His servants. He was careful to record communication with all kinds of people in order to emphasize the "whosoever will" nature of His Kingdom. He spoke to every category of person:

- *Men/women/children*
- *Godly men/ungodly men*
- *Kings/servants*
- *Rich/poor*
- *Jews/Gentiles*

In a day when women were considered property, God did not exclude them from His voice. He had significant communication with Adam and Abraham as well as their wives, Eve and Sarah.

At times God became creative in getting the ear of His people. He chose a bush for Moses (Exodus 3:4) and a donkey for Balaam (Numbers 22:28). One of His most dramatic methods was to use a hand materializing out of thin air to write on Nebuchadnezzar's wall (Daniel 5:1-30). He has ways and means to get our attention when there is a wax build-up in our ears.

The most startling mouthpiece God used to deepen relationship with His children was Jesus. He wanted His family to know the tone of His voice, not just His words. The best way to accomplish that goal was to send Jesus to earth for a season as a representative. Face time with a friend means so much more than an email. It is almost impossible to determine the tone of voice through written words alone.

Jesus' mission was to model God the Father in every aspect of His life on earth. Hebrews 1:3 says He is the express image of His person. He was such a perfect representation He could truthfully say, "He who has seen me, has seen the Father" (John 14:9). The record in the four Gospels of His three years of ministry on earth testified to His openness in talking with anyone and everyone, just like His Father.

At 12 He started His public life, talking with the religious leaders in the temple. His conversations were not limited to the synagogue. The next ministry event was a wedding reception, a stark contrast to the temple setting. At the wedding He demonstrated supernatural power by turning water into wine. A more startling aspect of the event was the Son of God mingling with men and women at such a non-religious gathering. God does not limit His communication to those with solemn faces in religious activities.

This was not the only secular event Jesus attended. The religious leaders were shocked by His choice of dinner companions. The local gossip was Jesus "eats with sinners and publicans" (Mark 2:16). It is doubtful they would have wanted to eat with Him if He spent the meal time exposing or condemning them as alcoholics, adulterers, or crooks. The author of Hebrews wrote that Jesus was anointed with the oil of gladness beyond His companions (Hebrews 1:9). I believe He was sought out because His presence brought life to any gathering. He was fun as well as profound. His mission was not to entertain people with His miracle-working power, but to woo them back to their Father by His demonstration of His love. Luke wrote "all the tax collectors and sinners drew near to hear Him." (Luke 15:1). From that report it doesn't sound like the sinners had any trouble hearing Him.

The Gospels present a cross-section of society being addressed by Jesus. The list includes tax collectors, military men, prostitutes, intellectuals, the uneducated, government officials, religious leaders, the homeless, wealthy, children, old and young men and women, fishermen, the helpless, the sick, and the dying. Jesus was so intent on communication with people that He even spoke to the dead. I am sure Lazarus was glad Jesus initiated that conversation by calling him to "come forth" (John 11:43). From the tomb his spirit responded to the familiar voice of his friend, Jesus.

Jesus had interaction with thousands of people during His three years of ministry. No smart-phone would have had enough memory to contain the list of His contacts. Of course it is possible to view the people on the list as ministry related rather than friends. As a public person in ministry, it is necessary to talk to people out of duty. Yes, I might have made it as one of the 5000 on His Facebook page, but that wouldn't mean He would communicate with me personally. Facebook friendship with a public figure would not be considered an intimate relationship. If He were choosing His close friend list, would I be on it?

Re-reading the character and qualifications of the disciples to whom He made the comment about His friendship gives me hope. Jesus either made a mistake in His selection of friends or He didn't have very high standards. He didn't require degrees, experience, testimonies of 40-day fasts, and total self-control of anger, jealousy, and deception. The disciples were more concerned about their own status, comfort, and future than His. The questions they asked must have challenged His patience, and yet He kept bringing them into His inner circle.

I have always been stunned by His willingness to share His last supper with the twelve. If it had been me, I would have left the men in the upper room, found a lovely quiet balcony overlooking the city, and enjoyed the Passover meal with John. The fact of His sharing such an intimate meal with the man who had already betrayed Him, as well as those who would deny even knowing Him, is incomprehensible. No matter how low men stoop in their sin, even sin against God Himself, He still wants to communicate with them.

At Jesus' baptism by John, His Father speaks from Heaven and says, "This is My beloved Son. Hear Him." (Mark 9:7). God never gives a command without providing the means to obey it. The matter of hearing is no different. First, God has given us not one, but *two* ears with which to hear. One would have been sufficient; however, He chose to accentuate hearing. We have equipment to catch the sound waves regardless of the direction from which they come. It is interesting to consider the fact we have two ears but only one mouth.

There are several instances in the Gospels where

Jesus heals people who are deaf. God installs the equipment and is also able to fix it (Matthew 11:5; Mark 7:32-37). Psalm 94:9 states that God formed the ear. Jesus demonstrated healing in every type of situation. The testimony of those healings is a source of inspiration to anyone who is sick. There is added encouragement for the healing of hearing problems because God puts such emphasis on our ability to hear.

The human body, as well as everything in the world, is held together by the Word of God. Hebrews 1:3 says He is "upholding all things by the word of his power." The atoms which make up our cells could not hold together without the moment-by-moment voice of God releasing waves of life-giving sound. We may have a difficult time consciously hearing the voice of God talking to us. It is encouraging to know the rest of our being is in constant communication with Him.

Jesus modeled hearing for us on several levels. First, He demonstrated God wants to talk to men on earth. The record in the four Gospels of His three years of ministry testifies to His eagerness to talk with everyone, just like His Father. Jesus was God but He functioned on earth as a man. He lived His life empowered by the Holy Spirit, just as we are to do. He knew when He prayed to His Father He was heard. More importantly, He knew His Father would speak to Him. The things Jesus said and did were a reflection of what He was seeing and hearing from His Father.

How comforting to know our Father is not like the gods of Baal and other Old Testament pagan gods. One of the most tragic pictures to me is the day Elijah confronted the prophets of Baal. He challenged them to prove the supremacy of their gods over the God of Israel. The prophets of Baal built their altar and called all day for fire to come down on the altar. The Bible record of this event states: "They called on the name of Baal from morning till noon, saying "Oh, Baal, hear us!" But [there was] no voice; no one answered. (I Kings 18:26). Our God is not silent. He demonstrated in the Old Testament and in the New Testament that He is a God who not only hears but speaks.

According to Romans 8:28-29, we are predestined to be conformed to the image of God's Son. That promise is relevant in terms of the issue of hearing God. Jesus knew the Father wanted to communicate with Him. His experience on earth proved that fact.

God was in constant communication with Him. We are told in I John 4:17 that "as He is, so are we in this world." We are to represent Him in the world. Without changing the original intent of Romans 8:28-29, one could say we are predestined to have our hearing conformed to the hearing of the Son of God. I John 4:17 would then be paraphrased to read "as He hears, so are we to hear in the world."

Satan devotes a great deal of time trying to short-circuit the connection between God and man because he knows how vital it is. He started the attack in the Garden of Eden and has continued to attempt to drive a wedge between man and God. He uses any lie that will cause us to believe God doesn't want to talk to us because He is busy with more important, perfect, intellectual, powerful people.

It is clear from all the Biblical evidence, the enemy would lose his case against God in a court of law. No one was ever shut out from God's voice. The Psalmist in Psalm 139 testifies to God being with him even in hell. We are beneficiaries of the fact He is the same yesterday, today, and forever. He will never lose His voice. He does not go on vacation and turn off His phone. He is never sick with laryngitis. He does not use the silent treatment on His children.

God is not picky about who, where, and when He communicates. He can't help Himself. He must talk. He *is* the Word.

His communication cannot be interrupted by anyone. No one has the power to turn off the Heavenly Internet connection, as has been done in some nations. He is like a radio broadcasting 24/7 over a powerful frequency. A radio is not selective regarding who may listen. Anyone who wants to hear may simply tune in.

THE MANY WAYS GOD SPEAKS

I would be thankful for a single radio station broadcast from God. True to His nature of creativity, He does not limit Himself to one station. God doesn't play just one type of music. How painful it would be if He only played country music and I was a classical music lover. He has many different stations which play a variety of sounds. God is able to broadcast sounds perfectly suited to my tastes, like the online radio stations that select music based on my preferences.

God is not one-dimensional, limited, or boring in His activities. His limitless creativity is evident whether looking at the individuality of a roomful of people or an aquarium filled with fish. I may not have seen all the fish God has created but that doesn't mean they don't exist, or that I might not see them in the future. In the same way, I may have a limited experience in hearing God. He is not governed by my lack of encounters with Him.

Our listening experience is expanded by having a list of available stations. If we know a station exists, we are more likely to listen for it as we surf the channels. It is equally helpful to know the various ways God may speak. I expand my hearing experience by listening in new directions. It is impossible to list all the ways God speaks because He cannot be reduced to a list. Every time we think we have identified His activities in totality, He surprises us with a new one. Balaam's ride on the talking donkey was undoubtedly totally unexpected. God can speak through anyone, anything, or even create something new if He wants to. A partial survey of ways He might speak is helpful if one understands He is a living, creative God who loves to expand our knowledge of Him.

BIBLE

The primary means of communication is the

Bible. All other communication will flow from and conform to it's foundational principles. The Bible is not merely black print on white pages. It is a living, God-breathed book. If reading it seems to be nothing more than a dry, boring textbook assignment, perhaps the reading is being done with the head and not the heart.

Hebrews 4:12

For the word of God [is] living and powerful, and sharper than any two-edged sword, piercing even to the division of soul and spirit, and of the joints and marrow, and is a discerner of the thoughts and intents of the heart.

GODLY PEOPLE

God's intent is to bring us together in a body. He often gives the word we need to someone else. We may pray, fast, and go through every spiritual hoop trying to get a word from God. If He wants us to hear Him through someone else, all of our efforts will be ineffective. The Holy Spirit is sent to expand our view outward beyond ourselves. If we have been hurt by others in the body, it feels safer to have a Jesus-and-me mentality. God will work to break down those walls, sometimes by giving the word I need to the most irritating person in the group, or someone less mature in the Lord. The offense is greater if the word from God comes through someone with a different theological viewpoint. The point is God speaks *through* the person. He can use a donkey if He needs to.

Hebrews 1:1

God, who at various times and in various manners spoke in time past to the fathers by the prophets...

2 Peter 1:21

For the prophecy never came by the will of man: but holy men of God spoke [as they were] moved by the Holy Ghost.

UNGODLY PEOPLE

God is not nervous speaking through unsaved people. The Bible is full of examples of ungodly people delivering a message from God.

Ezra 1:1

...the Lord stirred up the spirit of Cyrus king

of Persia, so that he made a proclamation throughout all his kingdom, and also [put it] in writing...

It is bad enough God chooses carnal Christians as His mouthpiece, but non-Christians? God may highlight to us the words of a secular newscaster or magazine. One sentence may be the answer to a question I asked God that morning. If I am open to the Holy Spirit, I will hear it. If I am operating in judgment of the person, I won't.

NATURE

Moses experienced the literal voice of God through the burning bush. Abraham had a life-changing encounter with God one night under the stars. The wise men "heard" God through the stars. That communication led them to the stable where Jesus had just been born. God's fingerprints are all over creation. Man has no excuse for rejecting God. He is speaking through His creation.

The problem comes when men put nature in the place of God. The focus of the occult is on the stars being the source of inspiration. The Christian emphasis is God and His Spirit speaking through the stars, as in the case of Abraham and the wise men. If I don't understand that distinction, I will either not allow God to give me an Abraham encounter or I will be drawn into the deception of putting faith in the daily horoscopes for direction rather than in God.

Romans 1:20

For since the creation of the world His invisible [attributes] are clearly seen, being understood by the things that are made, [even] His eternal power and Godhead, so that they are without excuse.

Psalms 19:1

The heavens declare the glory of God; and the firmament shews His handywork.

Exodus 3:2

And the angel of the Lord appeared to him in a flame of fire from the midst of a bush. So he looked, and behold, the bush was burning with fire, and the bush [was] not consumed.

VISIONS AND DREAMS

Visions and dreams are visual communication

from God either during the day or night. Both of them are "seen" rather than "heard" on the screen of our brain. Often people who say they don't see are merely looking in the wrong place. Perhaps if we called these encounters "mental pictures" it would bring it out of the spiritual stratosphere down to where most of us live.

Try this little test right now. At the end of this chapter there is a word in bold print. (Don't look now.) When you read the word, close your eyes. Once you have a picture of the word, open your eyes and write down the description of it under the word. When this test is done in a group, the results are fascinating. Usually very few people have "seen" the same thing and yet they all "saw" something.

(Now turn to the end of this chapter and read the word.)

The place where you "saw" the word is the same place you will look for the pictures or movies God wants to share with you. There is not a separate screening room for God's videos. There is only one canvas in your mind, which is why looking at pornography or very violent movies is not wise. If the screen was used for porn, there may be a fear of "looking" at it because of what might be playing. The result is I cut myself off from a major way God wants to "talk" to me.

The Bible records the dreams and visions of both believers and non-believers. Having God speak through those means is not a sign of great spirituality. The most carnal Christians on the planet have dreams and visions. If we believe those encounters are only for people more advanced in God, we limit God's ability to speak to us.

The promise of the Holy Spirit's outpouring carried with it the promise of dreams and visions. The Spirit was to be released on all flesh (Joel 2:28-29). It would be reasonable to assume if I am in the flesh, I am a candidate to receive a dream or a vision from the Spirit. The only requirement to experience either of these is to be in the flesh.

It is possible more non-Christians are aware of having dreams than believers. One evidence of the extent of the dream experience of pagans is the fact there are at least 17,000,000 dream interpretation sites on Google. The majority of them are not interpreting from a Christian perspective.

The sad fact is most pre-Christians rely on other non-Christians for the interpretation of a dream sent to them from God. Often Christians live with the mystery of a recurring dream. They spend money on dream interpretation classes, books, and dictionaries and still have no revelation of the meaning. When a person asks me to interpret a dream for them, my first response is: "Have you asked the Holy Spirit what the dream meant?" Invariably there is a moment of silence, a somewhat perplexed expression followed by a one-word answer: "No."

God's intention is not to tease us with a mysterious dream or vision. The same Spirit that brought the dream can interpret it. The experience of Daniel interpreting the king's dream should be a comfort and encouragement to all believers.

Daniel 2:23, 26-28

I thank you and praise you, O God of my fathers; You have given me wisdom and might. And have now made known to me what we asked of You, for You have made known to us the king's demand.

The king said to Daniel: "Are you able to make known to me the dream which I have seen and its interpretation?"

Daniel answered in the presence of the king, and said "The secret which the king has demanded, the wise[men], the astrologers, the magicians, and the soothsayers cannot declare to the king; but there is a God in heaven who reveals secrets, and He has made known to King Nebuchadndezzar what will be in the latter days. Your dream, and the visions of your head upon your bed, were these;..."

SENSES

When God speaks to us through our senses, it is easy to discount or even ignore the communication. Often the comment is made, "Oh, that was just my imagination" or "That's just me thinking that." Sometimes rather than give credit to God, we say "my intuition says." In each situation it was the Holy Spirit talking, giving us a sense, an impression, a knowing in our knower. A big part of hearing God is simply giving Him the credit rather than attributing our guidance to ourselves or to chance. He does not usually announce Himself first, saying: "Attention, please, this is God, I have something to tell you."

The story in Acts of Paul's dangerous journey on a ship to Italy records the impression he received from God about the trip.

Acts 27:10

{Paul} advised them saying: "Men, I perceive that this voyage will end with disaster and much loss...

There are numerous examples in the Gospels of Jesus having a sense about someone. He would describe something about a person he had no way of knowing except by the Spirit communicating to His spirit. One such encounter was between Jesus and the scribes. Jesus had just healed a sick man who had been lowered on a stretcher through the roof by his friends. Mark records the incident in chapter two.

Mark 2:8

And immediately when Jesus perceived in his spirit that they so reasoned within themselves, he said unto them...

Hebrews 5:14 talks about the need for us to have our senses trained. God wants to engage us with Himself on every level. The Psalmist said, "Oh taste and see that the Lord is good" (Psalm 34:8). There is the possibility of encountering God through the sense of taste. Jesus is spoken of as having a fragrance which would awaken the sense of smell.

I was attending a prayer meeting soon after being baptized with the Spirit. Gatherings such as this were a new experience for me. As I sat, eyes closed, humming the unfamiliar songs, I smelled an intoxicating fragrance. I was wearing perfume, but I knew the scent in the air was not mine. The scent distracted me for the rest of the evening. As soon as the meeting ended, I made a point of meeting as many people as possible, in order to find the person with the perfume. I had never smelled anything as captivating. No one seemed to carry the scent I smelled. This was puzzling to me.

Several weeks later, with a different group of believers, I smelled the same fragrance. My sniff test of everyone proved unsuccessful again. I shared the experience with someone who had been a believer much longer than I. She had had similar experiences and informed me the fragrance came from the presence of God in the room. If that fragrance could be bottled and sold, the maker would be a billionaire.

ANGELS

Throughout the Old and New Testament, God chose angels as a favorite means of communication with His children. Several of the most significant messages delivered to men came through angels. Mary received one from Gabriel concerning the birth of Jesus. The day of His birth was the occasion of another momentous message from the angels. They declared peace from God to the entire world.

Luke 2:10

Then the angel said to them, "Do not be afraid, for behold, I bring you good tidings of great joy which will be to all people."

People usually respond to the subject of angels one of two ways. One group is afraid of putting too much emphasis on angels. As a result of their fear, they avoid all contact. The other group puts them on a par with God. The key to balance in this or any area is to focus on God as the source of the communication rather than the means He uses.

As a teenager I knew very little about angels except from Sunday School Bible stories. Our church did not teach about present-day angelic experiences. If someone had asked me if I had ever seen an angel, my answer would have been "No!" until the day I had my tonsils taken out. I never liked visiting people in the hospital and was terrified at the prospect of being admitted for surgery. Because I hated hospitals, I never watched any of the medical TV shows. If I had, I might have had more knowledge of what to expect. I did know I wanted to be knocked out for the surgery. No one had told me how strange it would be to wake up from a general anesthesia.

I remember being half awake in a large room with bright lights. The moaning of other people around me was frightening. The surroundings were so unfamiliar I was unsure if I was still alive. My head was spinning. I tried to to get up but felt like a heavy blanket was holding me down. A warm hand grasped my clammy one and a sweet, melodious voice said, "Faith." The hand continued to hold my hand. Periodically, I saw a blurry smile gazing at me. Peace enfolded me.

The next time I woke up, I was back in my hospital room. Nurses came in and out, but no one had the smile of the person in the recovery room. Her comfort had touched me so deeply I wanted to meet her. My parents enquired about who attended to me after surgery. The answer they got was: "No one." I believe it is possible the "no one" was an angel sent to minister to me. (Hebrews 1:14).

THE VOICE OF GOD

God may choose to communicate directly by the "still small voice" (I Kings 19:12). This voice is in contrast to the reference in Matthew 3:17 of the audible voice of God from heaven as Jesus was being baptized or the voice out of the cloud on the Mount of Transfiguration described in Matthew 17:5. It is possible that as God manifests Himself in a group, one person will hear Him audibly; another will hear Him as the still small voice. In John 12:29, some people heard thunder; others heard the voice of an angel.

The voice of God highlights the most important aspect of the whole issue of hearing. Whether the bush, the donkey, the stars, or the angels are speaking, the source is the same. The words are coming from the heart of a loving Father. Furthermore, this is not just any Father, but the Father of Jesus Christ and because of that, our Father.

It is possible to become so caught up in the words (or prophecies) themselves that they become separated from their source. If we are more infatuated with the words than we are in love with the person speaking, we are more vulnerable to deception. Jesus said that sheep know the voice of their shepherd and follow him. They will not follow the voice of a stranger (John 10:1-5). Both shepherds may be calling the sheep with the same words. The knowledge of the shepherd's voice is the protection the sheep have against being led astray by strangers.

Jesus modeled this relational aspect of hearing. He exhibited confidence His Father would respond when He talked to Him, whether at a casual meal or during the traumatic night in the garden before His death. Heaven was always open. There was never any interference in the lines of communication. Every aspect of our life is the same as His, including intimacy with our Heavenly Father.

Anything God does will have the element of the supernatural attached to it. Our ability to hear is no different. Proverbs 20:12 says, "The hearing ear, and the seeing eye, the Lord has made them both."

Paul told the Corinthians in I Corinthians 2:14, "The natural man does not receive the things of the Spirit of God, for they are foolishness to him; nor can he know [them], because they are spiritually discerned."

God does not base His communication with us on our intellect, education, or theological training. He *gives us* everything we need. The most important gift is the Holy Spirit. As Jesus was preparing to leave, He told the disciples He would send the Comforter who would lead them into truth (John 16:13). He would take the things of God and give them understanding. All the various ways God has spoken to us in the past have their source of inspiration from the Holy Spirit.

WORD... HAMBURGER

Describe what you "saw" on the screen of your mind.

....

....

....

....

....

....

....

....

....

IF HE'S SPEAKING,
WHY CAN'T I HEAR?

The scriptures highlighted in previous chapters establish the undeniable fact God desires to talk to everyone. No one, living or dead, is excluded from the conversation. Initially this truth may not be good news if I don't hear God. As long as I could blame God, there was no pressure on me to fix the hearing problem. The good news is the communication breakdown can be remedied once the source of the problem is uncovered.

The importance of a proper diagnosis is illustrated by a story I heard about a man who was concerned about his wife's loss of hearing. He was afraid to confront her directly without confirmation his suspicions were correct. A friend suggested he stand about 12 feet away from his wife and ask her a question. He told him to move closer, asking the same question until she answered. This test would provide the evidence he needed.

The man took his friend's advice. When he returned home, his wife was standing in front of the stove, cooking. He stood 12 feet away from her and asked what she was cooking. She didn't answer. As his friend suggested, he moved three feet closer to her and asked the question again. There was still no answer. Finally, he stood three feet away and asked again. His wife wheeled around, looked him in the eyes, and said sharply, "For the third time, CHICKEN!" He realized the hearing problem was not his wife's but his own.

The solution for this man was to buy a hearing aid or be healed by God. It would be wonderful if we could buy a hearing aid at Walmart to fix our hearing problems. Unfortunately Walmart doesn't carry an appliance to fix our deafness. The diagnosis for our complaint would be in the heart rather than the ear. God told Ezekiel to receive in his heart the word (Ezekiel 3:13). Hearing God is more than a physical or mental activity. God communicates with us from His heart. His words are aimed at our heart. Any blockages in our heart will hinder our ability to receive His words.

It is normal for parents and children to have communication. You don't ignore a child's lack of responsiveness to your words. First you check to see if there is a physical problem with their ears. Next you do an attitude check. Is the child angry, depressed, or rebellious? The problem with the child's hearing is never fixed by a parent's impatience or anger. God does not condemn us for deafness. He is eager to resolve the issue because He longs for intimacy with us.

Two major influences contribute to spiritual deafness. Our difficulty in hearing God didn't start with us. It originated in the Garden of Eden. The result of Adam and Eve's sin was separation from God. Ephesians 2:12 refers to men after the apple incident in the garden as being "without God in the world." God was not just their Creator, but their Father. Father means source. As Creator He is the Source. In the Bible, the definition of the word "orphan" means *fatherless*. The effect of Adam and Eve's life without the Father continues today through the orphan spirit passed on from generation to generation. As orphans, they were excluded from the provision and protection of the Father's family.

From the day Adam and Eve were banished from the Garden, Father God set in motion His plan to restore relationship with man. Centuries passed before the reconciliation would be possible. Until that time Adam and Eve, as well as the succeeding generations, lived as orphans. The walk in the garden in the cool of the evening was a thing of the past. The intimate conversation between Adam and his Father ended.

In the meantime, the enemy continued to fertilize and water the lie that man would be better off on his own than depending on Father God. He portrayed Him as repressive, not having man's best interest at heart. Men and women bumbled along, doing the best they could. Generation after generation lived as orphans, experiencing the excruciating pain of fatherlessness.

Orphans live with deep, gnawing fears. The fear may be of:

- *rejection*
- *abandonment*
- *criticism*
- *judgment*

- *pain*
- *intimacy*

When rejection is experienced, it may produce a ripple effect of:

- *low self-esteem*
- *isolation*
- *defensiveness*
- *distrust*
- *performance*
- *perfectionism*

The list of emotions experienced by an orphan includes jealousy, competition, hoarding, striving, insecurity, anger, bitterness, resentment, elder brother syndrome, sense of being overwhelmed. An orphan does not have access to a father's wisdom in making decisions about the future. Fear of making a wrong decision may cause an orphan to seek direction from astrology. It is startling to see the number of websites offering "Christian" astrology or "Christian" horoscopes. The words "Christian" and "astrology" cannot possibly be used next to each other. They are from two different kingdoms. The fact there are so many websites indicates the number of Christians tormented by an orphan spirit. They feel disconnected from their Heavenly Father. This lack of intimacy hinders them from hearing advice and counsel from Him.

You may be thinking, "What does the orphan spirit have to do with my not hearing God?" The answer to that question is: "Everything!" If any attitudes of the orphan spirit are operative, they will not only affect relationships with family and friends, but also with God. An orphan's fear of being rejected or abandoned creates pressure to perform in order to maintain the relationship. The orphan must outperform anyone who is a legitimate child. This insecurity produces defensiveness against anyone (including God) who attempts to get close. Intimacy is feared because flaws might be seen, which would result in rejection.

The orphan spirit affects my ability to hear God in every area of life, including giving. I may not be able to respond if He tells me to put $100.00 in the Salvation Army bucket outside the grocery store at Christmas. As an orphan, I don't have the security of a father behind me. Everything I do depends on my own efforts. I cannot afford to risk giving away my grocery money for the week. The person living as a son or daughter has confidence in a loving Father as the source of everything. As a member of the family, I know Dad's voice. If He says put your grocery money in the bucket, I am confident He will provide for my needs.

The second major hearing hindrance is the religious spirit. While God was waiting to bring about the restoration of His children into the family, He established a set of rules to serve as a guide until the restoration was accomplished by Jesus Christ. The laws could never replace the personal guidance Adam had in the Garden but, as boundaries, provided some security. The world in Moses' day would have been a terrifying place to live without the security of a benevolent Father's presence. The people were afraid but did not want personal contact with God. They were happy for Moses to serve as their intermediary. The religious spirit was born when fear drove men to allow other men to stand between them and God.

Fear always leads to control. God's laws administered by fearful men, driven by a religious spirit, reduced men to slaves until Jesus Christ. Religion became the surrogate father for the orphans. Some of the fingerprints of the religious spirit are the same as the orphan spirit. Both of them use fear as a means of control. The religious spirit's control produces fear of:

- *condemnation*
- *rejection*
- *judgment*
- *punishment*
- *death*

The religious spirit causes men to be controlled by:

- *guilt*
- *shame*
- *perfectionism*
- *deception*
- *hopelessness*

The sense of belonging provided by the religious spirit to those with an orphan spirit seems worth the loss of freedom experienced under this surrogate father. Unfortunately, the price of relationship is performance. There is not the security of a blood relationship. You may be kicked out of your birth family's house, but you are forever part of that family. You didn't earn your place, you were born into it.

Religion says you can be part of the family only if you perfectly fulfill the requirements. Children in this family are kept in line by the pressure of guilt and shame as well as the threat of excommunication. The Holy Spirit is not welcomed by the religious spirit because He cannot be controlled. He does not conform to the traditional, safe, rigid rules of behavior established by the religious spirit.

The modern gang is an example of orphans being "adopted" into a family by a surrogate father ruling with a religious spirit. The "fathers" of the gang establish a set of rules. Membership in the gang provides security, relationship, and identity, similar to a family. However, in the gang your place "in the family" is secure only as long as you obey the rules. Expulsion and possible death are the result of disobedience.

The religious spirit operating among Judeo-Christians is not as violent as a gang leader, but just as controlling. The pressure to perform perfectly is constant. The nagging voice says "you haven't prayed enough" or "you should have fasted longer." It feels safer to cover up problems than bring them into the light, for fear of being judged and rejected. I believe the devastating failures of some high-profile ministers would not have happened if they had not been influenced by a religious spirit to hide their struggles for fear of being condemned and expelled.

Hebrews says coming to God is not based on behavior but on one thing: faith. "Without faith it is impossible to please [Him], for he who comes to God must believe that He is and that He is a rewarder of those who diligently seek Him." (Hebrewss. 11:6).

The orphan spirit whispers in our ear: "You don't have a father – a father doesn't exist for you so there's no way he will talk to you."

The religious spirit says, "You may have a father, but he is angry with you and it is not safe to have him talk to you, so avoid conversation with him."

Often the influence of both the orphan spirit and religious spirit are operating in a person's life without their knowledge. Just because a person becomes a believer and knows the Bible does not mean they are experiencing the fullness of a relationship with the Father. It is difficult to approach God in faith if I still believe the lie I don't have a Father or I have a Father who is angry with me.

I ministered to a man in a Sozo* session who had been extremely successful in business. He had lived a stellar life as a Christian, raised godly children, and now served as a missionary. In the course of the prayer session, I suggested he ask Father God what

He thought of him. As he did, I saw one large tear slowly roll down his face. I asked him what he was sensing. He said Father God had put His arm around his shoulder. Suddenly his whole body shook as he sobbed uncontrollably.

Through his tears he told me he heard Father God telling him how pleased He was with him. He said he had worked all his life to gain his father's approval. Never once had his dad affirmed him, much less embraced him. He grew up striving to perform perfectly. He kept hoping one day he would receive his earthly father's approval. The rejection he had felt from his dad made it difficult for him to believe God would accept him. As he left the office, still stunned by the encounter, he said he had taught about the Fatherhood of God for years but had never heard His voice until that moment. This man realized there is a huge difference between reciting the scripture that says I am adopted and actually hearing the Father's voice address us as His child.

The blockage in our hearing stems from lies. We may believe God doesn't want to talk to us because we had a sinful past and are not worthy. The block will not be removed by "being good" or punishing ourselves for "x" number of years until we feel worthy.

We will never have a "good" season long enough to feel worthy. The only solution is to renounce the specific lie we believe and ask God for the truth.

There may be several lies we believe that stem from the orphan or religious spirit. Hearing improves as we continue to renounce the lies and confess the truth God speaks to counter the lie. This simple action is as powerful as the most potent ear-flushing medicine available.

I have witnessed the power of God's truth bringing restoration of intimate communication with the Father as lies are renounced. I prayed with a woman who had suffered depression for years. During a prayer session, I learned she led a sinful life as a young woman. She had become a Christian, but never heard His voice or felt His love. Although she had asked God to forgive her many times, she had never forgiven herself. The moment she said, "I forgive myself and I receive your forgiveness, Father God," her world changed. She jumped up and danced around the room. For the first time she heard her Heavenly Father tell her she was forgiven.

Another woman I met with had had an abortion as a teenager. Her parents were not supportive, so she went through the experience alone. Later in life she became a Christian, but never experienced an intimate relationship with God. When the subject of the abortion came up, she asked Father God if there was any lie she believed about the experience that hindered her relationship with Him. After a few moments her lips began to quiver as tears poured out of her eyes. She said God was showing her the scene of the abortion in the clinic. Father God revealed to her He had been standing beside her throughout the abortion. Until that moment she had believed He was outside with the protestors. That lie had driven her to work hard trying to pay for her sin and earn God's acceptance. Although God didn't sanction the abortion, He didn't allow it to stop His love for her. She understood for the first time that nothing could separate her from the love of the Father.

The Bible says in Romans 8:15-16, "For you did not receive the spirit of bondage again to fear, but you have received the Spirit of adoption by whom we cry out, "'Abba, Father.'"

John 3:16 says that "God so LOVED the world that He gave His only begotten son."

Galatians 4:4-5 says, "But when the fullness of the time had come, God sent forth his Son, born of a woman, born under the law, to redeem those that were under the law, that we might receive the adoption as sons."

By combining the words of these scriptures, we can state the following truth:

Because God loved me, He sent His Son into the world, to save me from the fear and bondage of the law. He adopted me by His Spirit, who witnesses to my spirit I am no longer an orphan but the child of a loving Father.

Ask the Holy Spirit to show you any lie you may still believe about yourself or about God that would keep you from hearing His voice. Let Him show you anyone you need to forgive who might have been partially responsible for that lie taking root and robbing you. The Holy Spirit wants to give you truth in place of the lie, freedom instead of bondage, sonship in place of slavery.

Jesus told His disciples if they continued in the word, they would know the truth and the truth would set them free. The power behind the lies we believe is Satan, whom Jesus referred to as the father of lies. The power behind the truth is God. The reason the truth sets us free from the lies of the enemy is because our Father is a big God. The devil is powerless when confronted by Him.

* *Sozo is an inner healing and deliverance ministry. For more information:* www.bethelsozo.com

THE TONE
OF HIS VOICE

Once we experience adoption as a child of God and are set free from the bondage of the religious spirit of the law, we must learn the tone of His voice. Scripture is filled with references to the voice of God. However, not every reference to His voice sounds welcoming, safe, or comforting. Psalm 29 refers to His voice as powerful, breaking the cedars, dividing the flames, shaking the wilderness. His voice causes mountains to melt (Psalm 46:6). Sometimes His voice sounds like thunder, other times like a trumpet. None of these references encourage me to get to close to Him.

Through Jesus, His voice is heard calming storms,

speaking healing to the sick, inviting children to come to Him, releasing the woman caught in adultery from her sin. Lazarus came back to life at the sound of His voice. The picture of Jesus celebrating as a bridegroom at a wedding reception brings to mind sounds of joy, laughter, and singing.

There is a definite contrast between the references in these two paragraphs. Some of the images draw me closer to God; others make me want to protect myself from Him.

For many years I read the One Year Bible. Each day's reading included an Old and New Testament passage, Psalm, and Proverb. After reading the New Testament selection for the day, I felt the love, acceptance, forgiveness of God. That love generated hope and confidence to pursue my purpose. I would then read the Old Testament selection. The chapter for the day might be the account in Genesis of God's plan to kill man in a flood because of his evil heart. Suddenly my courage was gone. I knew my heart was not always obedient or pure. Would I go to sleep that night never to wake up again, having drowned in an unexpected flood brought on by my sin? I spent most of my Christian life swinging back and forth between two thoughts: God loves me; God is angry with me.

I am thankful for revelation that brought an end to my torment. It came through a statement by Bill Johnson, Senior Leader of Bethel Church in Redding, California. Sometimes the most profound moments are totally unexpected. Their full effect is not known until much later. The setting in this case was a question and answer session. I don't remember what question was asked. The important words for me were the response. Bill said, "Jesus is perfect theology. If Jesus isn't the answer to every question, then you are asking the wrong question." At the time my spirit resonated with the words, although I didn't know what they meant. I found myself quoting his statement because it felt true, even though I still didn't understand it.

Several months later, as I was reading the Old Testament passage for the day, I felt my stomach tighten, as if preparing for the judgment of God on my life. Suddenly I saw Jesus put Himself on the page at the place where God's anger was being meted out to the Israelites by their enemies. It clicked. I realized all God's anger, judgment, and punishment of man for his sins, including mine, was taken out on Jesus. The Jesus of Isaiah 53 was revealed on every page of the Old Testament.

Isaiah 53:4-6

Surely he hath borne our griefs, and carried our sorrows...But He was wounded for our transgressions, [He was] bruised for our iniquities...by His stripes we are healed.

I didn't have to live in fear of God's anger anymore. Jesus was not only the answer to every question, but to all fear and anxiety in regard to my relationship with God.

The tone of God's voice changed between the Old Testament and the New Testament. When Jesus was born, the voice of God spoke through a chorus of angels declaring the good news of peace on earth and good will from God (Luke 2:14). A cataclysmic shift happened as a result of His birth, death and resurrection. A new government was established which made it possible for man to be restored to God. Once we become believers, we must read the Old Testament from the position of being in Christ. There is no going back. The page has been turned. The Bible says the law and the prophets were "until John" (Luke 16:16). The word "until" signifies a line of demarcation that changed history. We are no longer orphans under bondage to a religious spirit.

The orphan and religious spirits may still have a measure of influence in our lives because of long association with them. We are in a process of having our senses trained as well as bringing every thought captive to the obedience of Christ. This means Jesus is perfect thinking as well as perfect theology. How I think about God will affect how I hear Him. If I read the Old Testament outside of Jesus Christ, it will be difficult to hear Father God speak lovingly to me.

It is significant the last words of the Old Testament speak about the restoration of the hearts of the fathers to children and children to fathers. Jesus made that miracle possible. First He modeled the loving heart of the Father during His life on earth. Then He offered Himself as the perfect sacrifice for all our sins. He became the bridge of reconciliation between the Father and His children as well as between every father and child on earth. Watching restoration between a believer and their Heavenly Father is a moving experience.

I prayed for a man who had grown up in an abusive house. He had chosen law enforcement as a career. His line of work added mortar to the walls he had put up to protect himself as a child from the rage of his dad. He had become a Christian but felt separated from God. He desperately wanted to hear God but wasn't sure God would want to talk to Him. During the prayer session he forgave his dad and asked the Holy Spirit to remove the walls that kept him from intimate relationships. He was literally thrown back in his chair as the power of God demolished the wall. He sat for a moment with his eyes closed. Tears began to stream down his cheeks. I asked him what he was hearing. He said Father God was hugging him, telling him how much he loved him. He had never heard his own father express love for him. The only physical touch he had felt from his dad had been in the form of beatings.

On another occasion I met with a career military officer. He had grown up in a chaotic alcoholic home. As a young man he joined the military to escape his father's abusive tirades. No matter how hard he tried, he was never able to please his dad. His efforts were met with criticism, disapproval, and rejection. He spent his career trying to prove himself by taking the most dangerous assignments. Although he had become a Christian, he related to God as a commanding officer rather than as his Father. He felt God's acceptance as long as he won medals and received promotions.

While serving in a foreign country, away from his wife and family, he committed adultery. He was devastated by what he had done. The damage to his marriage seemed irreparable. The guilt and shame were unbearable. Because of this moral failure, he felt he could not even approach God.

His picture of God was colored by his experience of his father's demand for the perfection he could never deliver. God's voice in his ear always sounded angry like his dad's. He finally mustered enough courage to face God and ask His forgiveness. As he did, he saw an instant replay in his mind of his sin. He was shocked to see Father God in the room as the event took place. The sight of tears in God's eyes stunned him even more. There was no anger, condemnation, or rejection coming from Him, only a Father's love for a hurting son. That day the tone of God's voice in his ear changed.

A checklist in our mind of the distinguishing marks of the tone of Father God's voice is important. It helps filter out the lingering lies from the orphan and religious spirits.

The tone of His voice will always be marked by:

- *forgiveness*
- *acceptance*
- *encouragement*
- *strengthening*
- *hope*
- *love*

Whenever we sense negative words which tear down with:

- *condemnation*
- *rejection*
- *discouragement*
- *judgment*
- *hopelessness*
- *accusation*

we know the words are not coming from our Father. Two truths are powerful weapons against the enemy's attempt to confuse. The first truth is we are not orphans under the cruel taskmaster of the law. Second, we are sons and daughters of a loving Father whose heart is always open to us because of Jesus Christ.

EAR TRAINING

The word "practice" may seem out of place in relationship to the subject of hearing God. However, the Bible is replete with references to training, endurance, perseverance, and diligence in the pursuit of God. Our society is enamored with and addicted to the instantaneous. Patience is not required in a technological world of nanosecond downloads. The idea of spending time to acquire a skill is not popular. If we can't immediately master the skill required for a game on the Wii or an app on the iTouch, it is easier to move on to a new one than press on to success. Why continue pursuing something which doesn't provide immediate satisfaction or reward? Applying this philosophy to the Christian life results in some believers shelving the goal of intimate communication with God, along with such things as prayer, fasting, signs, and wonders, with the comment, "I tried that but it didn't work."

There are still a few areas of life where repetition and time are unavoidable. One endeavor is learning to speak and understand a foreign language. Memorizing a vocabulary list does not enable a person to function in that language. Part of learning the language is spending hours each week in the language lab listening to a person speak the words. Without learning the sounds and inflections, it is possible to make some embarrassing mistakes when trying to speak. One wrong accent on a word can mean the difference between applause and boos.

Hearing God accurately also requires spending time in His language lab, learning His vocabulary as well as the tone of His voice. There are several activities that rapidly increase our capacity to understand His language.

SOAKING

Soaking in His presence is the best place to become familiar with His Voice. If possible, carve out time each day to spend alone with Him. It is not the time to bring a laundry list of things you want done in the world or even in your own life. There is a big difference between a work day and date night. It is not wise to bring discipline problems with the children or budget shortfalls into an intimate time with a spouse. Most relationships are strained if one person always wants something or does all the talking. Of course God forgives us for treating Him like a vending machine. He much prefers spending time with us rather than our list.

The atmosphere and activity of Heaven may be a surprise to some. If one doesn't get to know Father God, Jesus, and the Holy Spirit on earth, Heaven may be a shock. As my mother's moving date to Heaven drew closer, she expressed concern about whether she would fit in. She had a great sense of humor. She said she sometimes suffered with humor until she was free to let loose one of her one-liners. To allay her fear, I read her Psalm 126:1-2. The Psalmist wrote: "When the Lord turned again the captivity of Zion, we were like them that dream, then was our mouth filled with laughter, and our tongue with singing..." She was relieved to know there would be much laughter in Heaven. She knew she would feel at home.

Throughout the Bible God expresses His desire for us as His children to know Him. I don't believe He is referring to knowing facts about Him to use in a Bible Trivia game. He wants us to be acquainted with all the glorious aspects of His being, including His laugh. I believe it is possible to hear the sound of God's laugh as we soak. Psalm 2 says that "God sits in the Heavens and laughs." Ephesians 2:6 says we are "seated together in Heavenly places" with Jesus. Unless I have a hearing problem, I would imagine His laugh would be loud enough for me to hear if I am sitting with Him.

THE LIVING BIBLE or THE MESSAGE

Both the Living Bible and The Message are powerful translations that bring the Bible to life with the help of the Holy Spirit. Sometimes we have become so familiar with the scriptures it is difficult to avoid being lulled to sleep as we read. Obviously the problem is with us and not God. It helps to find ways to bring new life into reading the Bible. The enemy enjoys watching Christians give up on scripture reading because it has become a duty rather than the source of daily bread it was intended to be. Religious duty has robbed many of the life-giving dimensions of Bible reading. The biggest excitement some believers have is checking the box that shows the reading assignment for the day has been done.

I think a supernatural encounter with God in the midst of the book of Kings or Joshua would be a great Bible-reading session. What if the page opened up and you were on the field watching Elijah call down fire from heaven? You might come away from that chapter with singed eyebrows.

Pray that the Presence that was on the word as it was spoken would come on you as you read. The fact that our experience reading does not match that of the people who heard it live is not because of the passing of centuries. The word is living. The same spirit that breathed those words into the speaker lives in us.

As a college student I had the privilege of spending time with Derek and Lydia Prince, two of the great generals in the Body of Christ. One evening I was sitting next to Lydia in a meeting as Derek preached. I had heard the message numerous times before. My mind began to wander as my body struggled to stay awake. Periodically I glanced at Lydia. She was totally engaged in his words. I sensed the presence of the Holy Spirit around her as she prayed softly in the Spirit under her breath. At the end of the meeting Lydia was as radiant as if she had just had an encounter with the Holy Spirit. She turned to me and said, "I have heard this many times but the Holy Spirit always makes it new. I always hear something I have never heard before." Lydia knew the Holy Spirit was the key to hearing God's voice through the scripture. The word was alive to her.

SPEND TIME WITH PEOPLE WHO HEAR GOD

My experience with Lydia Prince and people like her helped me grow in my ability to hear God. I watched her interaction with the Holy Spirit in different settings. The relationship she had was not stiff but relaxed, as with a friend.

It is possible to gain as much benefit from a person by watching them receive from God as it is to draw out of them what they have received. Eating a delicious fresh fish dinner with the fisherman who just caught the fish is a treat. Learning to fish by watching the master fisherman at work is the key to a life of feasts.

Paul told the Thessalonians he was a "model for [them] to imitate" (2 Thessalonians. 3:9 NIV). To fulfill this directive from him, the readers of his epistles would need to observe Paul as well as read the letter. Sometimes association with the other person's anointing enables us to function in the zone in which they live in a way we have not done on our own. To duplicate that experience out of their realm would require practicing the principles learned from an observation of their life.

ASK GOD QUESTIONS and LISTEN FOR THE ANSWER

Our Father is the one person in the world who never becomes irritated by our questions. Just the opposite is true – He is delighted by our interest. The primary goal of God is relationship with us. He does not withhold things from us out of meanness. He wants our need to draw us to Him. He is the provision for every need and has the answer for every question. At the end of this book are several blank pages for questions and answers. Get a conversation started with God by writing down every question you have always wanted to ask but never did. Over the next weeks, review the questions. You don't want to miss God's answer because you forgot the question.

When God answers a question, we learn a little bit more about His heart. The more we know His nature, the easier it becomes to recognize His voice. A false assumption about His nature may cause us to blame Him for something that is not His doing. It is wiser to spend time asking questions and learning His ways than coming to a conclusion based on our experience with men. He is not like any human being we have ever met. Numbers 23:19 states "God [is] is not a man, that He should lie."

I was traveling with friends on a long overseas flight. One member of our group was in First Class. At one point during the flight, our friend came back to chat with us. He said, "I came earlier in the flight but you were asleep." I laughed and said, "I bet I was drooling and snoring loudly. I hope you didn't take my picture and post it on Facebook." With a hurt expression on his face he said, "I would never do that." I realized I had made an assumption about his behavior based on my experience with other people, rather than on his character, which was vastly different. I believe there are times God is as shocked by our misunderstanding of His nature as was my friend.

TAKE NOTE

...of the answers you hear to your questions. The

easiest way to do that is to write it down at the time. Journaling with paper and pen is the most familiar means of taking note of what God says. If you like to journal, it is helpful to find the right size, shape, color to use. After spending time and money looking for the perfect place to record God encounters, I ended up using the inexpensive, black-and-white, paper-bound composition book available at the grocery store. The engraved, leather bound one sat on the shelf. Every aspect of relationship with God should be comfortable, not awkward.

A smart-phone is a solution for those who have an aversion to writing. No matter where I am, I usually have my phone. Yes, I sleep with it. If I have a dream or revelation from God in the middle of the night, I reach for the phone, push the record button, and make voice notes. I don't need to fumble in the dark with pen and paper or wake myself up by turning on a light.

I know many people who keep their phones on "pause," ready to record any prophetic word that is given to them. No telling what might happen if we were that poised to record God's words to us. The time we take to preserve communication from God shows Him we have value for it. I am more willing to share deep things with a friend who shows interest by listening intently and remembering my words. As I show God I view His words as a treasure, it will encourage Him to reveal even more to me.

THE POWER
OF DESIRE

Our lives are on a fast track in today's society. Taking time to pause and reflect is challenging. Significant events are not savored because we have to "eat" or experience them on the run. It is tragic to use a fancy restaurant gift certificate for a take-out meal to eat in your car between appointments. The meal was meant to be memorable. Unfortunately, it may only be remembered because of the stain on your clothes from the bite you dropped as you rounded a corner.

Some of God's gifts of Himself are lost in the clamor and clutter of our lives. At the end of the book is a partial list of ways God may have spoken to you in the past. Take a few minutes to read the list. Check off the ways you have heard Him. Think about those encounters. Thank Him again.

There may be some items on the list that are unchecked. Circle the ones you desire to experience. The hand writing on the wall is one on my list. Hunger and thirst for God are keys to unlock more of His nature. The difference between those who experience intimacy with God and those who don't can be summed up in one word: DESIRE. God has unlocked the door to His heart. It is up to us to open it. Don't let a lie keep you from experiencing the fullness of intimate communication with your Father. He adores you and can't wait to tell you His secrets.

THE
EMPTY CHAIR

eligion de-personalizes God, reducing Him to rules, principles, laws and feel-good Bible stories for kids. Even aspects of God's character are separated from Him and become a commodity to be acquired through religious activity. Faith, hope, love, peace are a few of the aspects of His nature that are sought after.

In the midst of seeking God for help dealing with all our needs, fears, desires, we overlook the fact that God might have some desires Himself. We may have concluded that since He is God, He has everything He needs and wants.

Religion's focus is always dealing with our sin.

Even after the salvation experience, the spotlight is still on the issue of sin. The Christian life becomes a legal transaction void of emotion. The truth is God's desire was much bigger than taking care of our transgressions. Our guilt had to be addressed in order for His real goal to be reached, which was getting His children back.

The disobedience of Adam and Eve in the Garden affected not only them, but also the Father. I believe He looked forward all day to the evening walk in the garden with Adam. Religion would view those meetings as the boss checking up on Adam's work, making sure he had done everything perfectly. The Truth is the Father created Adam and Eve for fellowship with Himself. He sacrificed His son Jesus because of love for His lost children. He missed them.

The Tabernacle in the Old Testament was built as a prophetic statement of God's desire to dwell with His children. God told Moses, "Let them make me a sanctuary, that I may dwell among them" (Exodus 25:8). It would be the height of dysfunction for God to move in with His family and never talk to them. Many of us have grown up in a home with an absent or silent dad. The idea of a stay -at -home dad who wants to be with us is foreign.

Jesus had several assignments on earth. One important mission was modeling the Father. At one point in His ministry, Philip, one of the disciples asked Jesus to show him the Father. Jesus told him that if Philip had seen Jesus, he had seen the Father (John 14:8-9). On another occasion, as Jesus prayed He told His Father that He had revealed the Father's name (John 17:6). Every aspect of the Father's nature was demonstrated by Jesus as He ministered with love, mercy, forgiveness, joy, hope, peace, and power.

As his earthly ministry was coming to an end, he gathered with His disciples in an upper room for the their last supper. Although this dinner coincided with the Jewish calendar of Passover, Jesus was not hosting this event out of duty alone. He was not dispassionately enduring John leaning into him, resting his head on His chest.

Jesus said to the 12 disciples, including Judas, "with fervent desire I have desired to eat this super with you" (Luke 22:15). The Greek word for desire has a strong intensity of passion associated with it. Even greater emphasis is added to the statement because the word "desire" is used twice.

Jesus spoke to them about the future. He told

them He was going to the Father's house to prepare a place for them. We know we will be invited to the wedding feast. There is a seat with our name on it. We would be missed if we didn't show up. The Father has been waiting a long time to throw that party.

I believe the Father is not focused solely on that future event. He feels loss now when we allow fear, guilt, shame, self-hatred, to block us leaning into Him like John. I know this from personal experience.

Because my life had gotten busy, I was not spending as much time talking with Father God as I had in the past. Realizing what had happened, I asked Him to forgive me for neglecting Him. I had taken Him for granted. Of course He forgave me. As He did, He lovingly said, "I've missed you."

I picture Him sitting in a rocking chair on His porch, surveying the vast expanse of the universe. Beside Him is an empty chair, waiting for me to come rock with Him. Who knows what mysteries He has to share, wisdom to impart or songs to sing over me. I am not sure I will ever know the depth of joy He receives from our conversations together. The miracle of His porch is that there is a chair for each one of us.

QUESTIONS

ANSWERS

HEARING INVENTORY

Reading Bible

Christian Music

Spouse

Christian Friend

Boss

Stranger

Christian Book

Non-Christian Book

Creation (sunset/stars)

Piece of Art (Photo/Painting

Billboard

Phenomenon of Nature

God's Audible Voice

A Dance

Laying on of Hands

Prophetic Word

Still Small Voice

Feeling in your Body

Taste

Hand Writing on Wall

A Sermon

Parents

Siblings

Non-Christian

Co-Worker

Secular Song

Secular Movie

Christian Movie

Circumstances

Angel

Testimony

Dream

Impression

eMail/Card

Tongues

A Touch

Vision

Fragrance

Trance

Burning Bush

ADDITIONAL RESOURCES
from Faith

Instrumental Soaking CDs by Faith Blatchford

Age To Come

Mysteries

Age To Come – volume 3

Be Healed! – healing encounter with music/ scripture available in English, Spanish, Mandarin

Books

Soaking 101

Teaching CDs/DVDs

Outrageous Optimism

Freedom from Fears

Can You Hear Me Now?

Women Set Free

Speak to the Storm

Shifting Nightmares to Dreams

Unblocking Writer's Block

Get Faith's resources at:
www.FaithBlatchford.com or www.ibethel.org